P9-CBF-521

# The California Gold Rush

# The California Gold Rush

### Dennis Brindell Fradin

**Marshall Cavendish**
Benchmark

New York

Marshall Cavendish Benchmark
99 White Plains Road
Tarrytown, New York 10591-5502
www.marshallcavendish.us

Library of Congress Cataloging-in-Publication Data
Fradin, Dennis B.
The California Gold Rush / by Dennis Brindell Fradin.
p. cm. — (Turning points in U.S. history)
Summary: "Covers the California Gold Rush as a watershed event in U.S.
history, influencing social, economic, and political policies that shaped
the nation's future"—Provided by publisher.
Includes bibliographical references and index.
ISBN 978-0-7614-3012-4
1. California—Gold discoveries—Juvenile literature.  2. Gold mines and
mining—California—History—19th century—Juvenile literature.
3. California—History—1846–1850—Juvenile literature.  I. Title.
F865.F78 2008
979.4'04—dc22
2007030451

Photo research by Connie Gardner

Cover Photo: An illustration of gold miners from an 1856 magazine
Title Page: A Currier and Ives lithograph depicting California gold mining, 1871
Cover photo by Bettmann/CORBIS

The photographs in this book are used by permission and through the courtesy of: *The Granger Collection:* 3, 8, 13, 20, 24, 26, 37, 38, 42-43;
*Corbis:* Roger Wood, 6; Bettmann, 9, 12, 23, 27; *North Wind Picture Archives:* 16, 18, 28, 30, 32, 34

Editor: Deborah Grahame
Publisher: Michelle Bisson
Art Director: Anahid Hamparian

Printed in Malaysia
1 3 5 6 4 2

# Contents

A gold sculpture found in the tomb of King Tutankhamen. The figure, called a *selket*, is guarding the container of the king's mummy.

# CHAPTER ONE

# The Gleaming Yellow Metal

People have valued gold highly since ancient times. The gleaming yellow metal is valuable for two reasons. First, it is rare compared to other **substances** on Earth. Second, gold is beautiful. For thousands of years it has been used to make jewelry and other luxury items.

Golden ornaments dating back about six thousand years have been unearthed at Varna, Bulgaria. These ornaments are among the world's oldest golden objects made by human beings. The ancient Egyptians buried their kings with treasures of gold. For example, **archaeologist** Howard Carter found 2,500 pounds of golden objects in the tomb of King Tutankhamen, who ruled Egypt more than 3,300 years ago.

A third-century A.D Persian golden coin

Gold has also been used as money for a long time. The first known golden coins were made more than 2,600 years ago. They were used in the kingdom of Lydia in what is now Turkey.

Gold has inspired popular sayings such as "All that glitters is not gold" and "the pot of gold at the end of the rainbow." People have told many stories and legends about gold. In one

## From Lead to Gold?

Centuries ago, people had a strong desire to make gold. This desire inspired a false science called alchemy. Alchemists used secret powders, potions, and other materials to try to change one substance into another. For example, some alchemists said they could turn lead and other less valuable materials into gold. Alchemists could not actually make gold, but their work had other positive results. As they experimented with various substances, they helped begin the science of chemistry.

ancient Greek tale, King Midas wishes that everything he touches will turn to gold. He gets his wish. To this day, skilled businesspeople are said to have the Midas touch.

Gold is so precious that people flock to places where it has been found. They hope to strike it rich. This is known as a gold rush. One of the first gold rushes in the United States happened after gold was found near Dahlonega, Georgia, in 1829. The country's most important gold rush occurred about twenty years later in California.

King Midas watching his daughter turn to gold

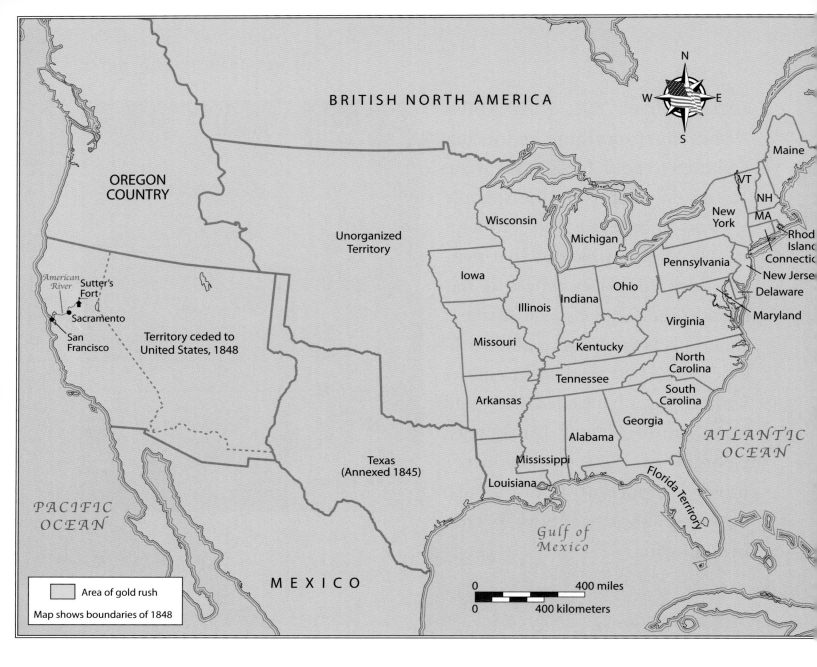

This map shows the boundaries of the twenty-nine states and the area of the Gold Rush in 1848.

# CHAPTER TWO

# "I Was Certain It Was Gold"

As the year 1848 began, the United States consisted of twenty-nine states. Nearly all of them were located in the nation's eastern half. At the time, the U.S. **population** was only 22 million—about one-thirteenth of what it is today.

California was not yet a state in 1848. In fact, at the start of that year, California did not yet belong to the United States. Mexico, the country just south of the United States, claimed California as its own. Not including Native Americans, California's entire population was just 15,000. Only a few thousand of these people were Americans. Most of the rest were of Mexican and Spanish heritage.

James Marshall, one of Sutter's best workers, made the discovery that started the rush for gold in the Sierra Nevada foothills of California.

On Monday, January 24, 1848, California was changed forever. James Marshall and his crew were building a sawmill along the American River near present-day Sacramento. Marshall was out looking over the tailrace—a small canal that carried water from the mill to the river. Suddenly the morning light shone on a yellowish gleam beneath the water. Marshall was curious. He reached into the cold water and picked up a yellow object smaller than a pea.

"It made my heart thump," Marshall later recalled, "for I was certain it was gold."

Marshall decided to show his discovery to John Sutter, a wealthy rancher and trader who owned the sawmill Marshall was building. Marshall found his boss at

## A Penniless Prospector

James Wilson Marshall was born in New Jersey. As a young man he headed west and tried settling in Indiana, Illinois, Missouri, and Oregon. He finally ended up in California. Marshall worked as a carpenter for John Sutter. For a time he was very successful. He bought a ranch, but then his cattle were stolen and he had to give it up.

Marshall made a deal with Sutter. Marshall would oversee construction of Sutter's sawmill at Coloma, California. In return, Sutter would give Marshall some of the mill's lumber. Strangely, Marshall's discovery of gold was disastrous. All the men in the area went off looking for gold, so the mill failed. Marshall also tried prospecting, but he wound up penniless. He spent his last days living in a small cabin. Poor and forgotten, the man who began the gold rush died in Kelsey, California, at the age of seventy-four.

James Marshall (1810–1885)

Sutter's Fort in what is now the city of Sacramento. The two men looked up the word *gold* in an encyclopedia. They also performed a few tests on the mysterious object. Their reading and testing removed all doubt. The substance was gold.

Over the next several days, sawmill builders and other people began searching the region for gold. They found more of it. Word spread that gold had been discovered at Sutter's sawmill. On March 15, 1848, the *Californian*, a newspaper based in the little town of San Francisco, ran the first story about the gold strike. The article was titled GOLD MINE FOUND.

Soon after, the *California Star*, another San Francisco paper, printed a story about the discovery. Samuel Brannan, editor of the *Star*, went to Sutter's sawmill and collected a bottleful of gold. On May 12 Brannan went through the streets of San Francisco. He held up his bottle for all to see and shouted, "Gold! Gold! Gold from the American River!"

Thanks to newspaper stories and word of mouth, a gold rush began in the spring of 1848. At first, nearly all of the **prospectors** came from within California. Many people dropped whatever they were doing to hunt for gold. It was said that San Francisco's school closed, and the teacher took his students to look for gold along the American River. Rumor spread that the town jailer of San Jose, California, released his prisoners so they could help him prospect.

## An Unlucky Strike

Johann Augustus Sutter (1803–1880) was of Swiss heritage but was born in Germany. By the age of thirty-one, Sutter was deeply in debt. He left his wife and children in his brother's care and rushed across the ocean. Sutter worked as a trader in Missouri, Oregon, Hawaii, and Alaska before he settled in California. In the United States he became known as John Sutter.

In 1841, Sutter was granted 48,827 acres (19,760 hectares) of land near today's city of Sacramento. He began a settlement called New Helvetia, which means "New Switzerland." Sutter became a rich rancher and trader. Soon his wife and four children left Germany and joined him in California.

The discovery of gold at his mill led to Sutter's downfall. His land grant did not include the place where the discovery occurred, so he had no right to the gold. Even worse, gold miners stole his animals and destroyed his fields of crops. Sutter became bitter about losing most of his fortune. He died at the age of seventy-seven.

Prospectors crossed rough terrain and faced danger of Indian attacks on the journey to California's goldfields.

The news reached the Mexican state of Sonora, and hundreds of people began walking to California. Gold hunters also arrived from as far away as Oregon and Hawaii. Before 1848 ended, five thousand prospectors were searching for gold in a region 200 miles (322 kilometers) long and 50 (80 km) miles wide in northern and central California.

Some prospectors struck it rich. Near Sutter's sawmill, a man dug out gold **nuggets** from beneath the doorstep of his house. They were worth $2,000—about $50,000 in today's money. Five prospectors on the Feather River found $75,000 worth of gold—equal to nearly $2 million today. A fourteen-year-old boy from Monterey, California, found $3,500 in gold on the Mokelumne River. This amount is equal to about $90,000 today. Another prospector was resting on a yellowish rock. Suddenly he realized something amazing—the rock was made of gold.

Even after all these success stories, the greatest gold rush days were still to come.

Wagons carrying Forty-Niners and their belongings often overturned on the steep trails, and their animals sometimes collapsed and died from exhaustion.

# CHAPTER THREE

# The Forty-Niners

Compared to today, news and people traveled slowly in the mid-1800s. As a result, it took a year for the California gold rush to get going in a huge way. By 1849, much of the world knew about California gold. Thousands of people caught what was called gold fever or California fever. About 85,000 people flocked to California in 1849 in search of riches. Because of the year, they were called Forty-Niners.

Many Forty-Niners traveled overland to California. The trip by wagon took about six months and covered 2,000 miles (3,219 km). Their wagons were often packed to the point of overflowing, so many Forty-Niners walked the whole way alongside their vehicles.

Other Forty-Niners came by ship. Two main sea routes linked the East Coast with the land of gold. The longer route went all the way around South America's southern tip to California. It covered 14,000 miles (22,531 km) and took roughly half a year to complete. Another route took people down to Panama. They crossed the narrow country and continued by ship to California. This route covered 6,000 miles (9,656 km) and took about three months.

Thousands of travelers never reached the goldfields. Accidents, disease, shipwrecks, and other hardships claimed their lives. However, thousands of others arrived safely in California. The Forty-Niners who came from the United States included some African Americans. Forty-Niners also came from dozens of

The cover of a California Gold Rush guide, published and sold for twelve-and-a-half cents in 1849

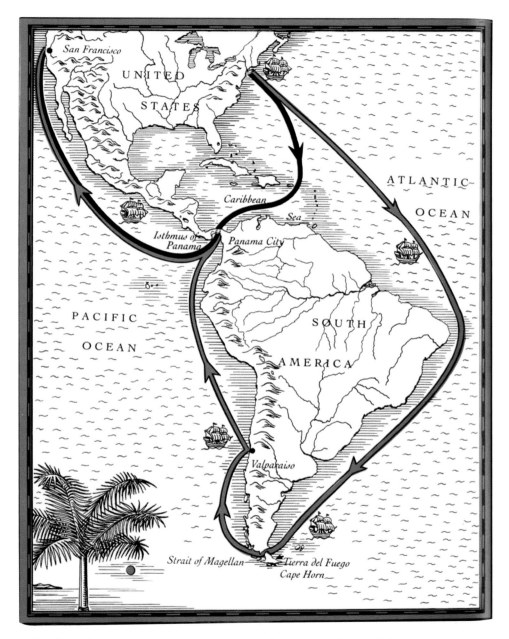

Whether the sea route was short or long, travel conditions were crowded and ticket prices were high—between three hundred and five hundred dollars.

other countries, including Mexico, Chile, Peru, Ireland, Germany, France, England, Australia, New Zealand, China, and Japan.

At first, many new arrivals lived in canvas tents or even in caves. Over time, mining camps formed in places where there was gold. These settlements had colorful names—Bed Bug, You Bet, Mad Mule Gulch, Red Dog, Shirt Tail Canyon, Rough and Ready, Fleatown, Humbug Canyon, Git-up-and-Git, and Hangtown.

The Forty-Niners generally did **placer mining**. This involved prospecting in beds of streams—sometimes dry streambeds.

Miners typically **panned** for gold. They filled metal pans with sand, gravel, and (they hoped) gold. Then they mixed this material with water. Gold is heavier than the other substances, so it sank to the bottom of the pan.

## *Pants for Panning*

Levi Strauss (1829–1902) was born in Germany. He lived in New York City as a young man. During the California Gold Rush, he moved to San Francisco and became a merchant. Levi Strauss made sturdy pants for miners, and they became very popular. Today, millions of people wear these pants. They are known as Levi's, or jeans.

Many prospectors used **cradles**, also called rockers. These devices were about five feet in length. Prospectors shoved material from a streambed into the cradle and added water. As prospectors rocked their cradles, slats at the bottom of the contraptions caught the gold.

Miners who "hit paydirt" just found tiny grains of gold called gold dust. They had to gather large amounts of gold dust to make much money. Every Forty-Niner's dream was to discover giant golden nuggets.

This photograph shows a miner in Tuolumne County using a rocker to catch tiny bits of gold.

Forty-Niners eagerly weigh their gold using a small scale.

# CHAPTER FOUR

# Fabulous Finds and Broken Hearts

Before the California Gold Rush ended in about 1857, there were many fabulous finds. The largest gold nugget was reported to weigh in at 160 pounds. It was worth $30,000—roughly $750,000 today.

Many prospectors found gold nuggets in the region around Columbia, California. One 300-acre (121-hectare) area at Columbia held $55 million in gold. That amount would equal more than a billion dollars in today's money.

Near Mariposa, California, a group of Mexican miners dug out $217,000 worth of gold—more than $5 million today. Discoveries like this inspired a legend back on the East Coast. People marveled that California was one solid hunk of gold.

An artist's view of Columbia, California in 1852

The truth did not quite match the legend. Most miners were lucky to find fifty dollars worth of gold in a week. Fifty dollars was hardly a fortune, but it was still a lot of money. At this time, a ten-dollar weekly salary was considered good. There was a new problem, however. The new wealth of the gold rush drove prices way up in California. Even on fifty dollars a week, prospectors had trouble making a **profit**.

**Merchants** charged sky-high prices for two reasons. First, goods often had to be shipped long distances to California. Second, merchants also hoped to get rich by "mining the miners." For example, a merchant might charge a miner two hundred dollars for a horse that would have cost ten dollars before the gold rush. Miners paid six dollars for a simple mining

A hotel or motel, Forty-Niner-style, could mean a space in a sheep corral to stretch out and rest.

pan and up to sixty dollars for a cradle. At Sutter's Fort, blankets sold for about seventy dollars each. Food was also extremely costly. In the gold-fields, a single egg could cost three dollars. An onion might cost two dollars.

For recreation, gold miners gambled and drank in smoke-filled saloons.

Even worse, gold began to lose much of its buying power. Miners often paid for items with gold because it was so plentiful. Soon, gold that had been worth eighteen dollars per ounce dropped to ten dollars per ounce or less.

Miners' gold disappeared in plenty of other ways. In every mining camp, saloons and gambling halls sprang up, and prospectors spent and lost great quantities of gold. Crooks lured miners with fake get-rich schemes. California Gold Grease was one scheme. Miners were supposed to buy this grease, cover themselves with it, and roll down a hill. As they rolled, schemers promised, gold would stick to their bodies.

Many prospectors were disappointed when they did not find the pot of gold at the end of the rainbow. They returned home. Others fell victim to poor diet, disease, or mining accidents. It is estimated that one of every six gold seekers died within a few years of arriving in California.

General Zachary Taylor led his troops to victory during the Mexican War. Taylor later became twelfth president of the United States.

# CHAPTER FIVE

# The Thirty-first State

The gold rush happened at a **crucial** time in California history. When James Marshall found gold at Sutter's sawmill, a war was about to end. People in the United States called it the Mexican War (1846–1848). The United States fought the war to obtain lands ruled by Mexico. Just nine days after Marshall's discovery, the Mexican War ended with the signing of a treaty. According to this agreement, Mexico gave a great deal of land to the United States. This land included California.

Most U.S. **territories** had to wait a long time before becoming a state. Things moved much faster in California, largely because the area's population soared during the gold rush. By 1850, California's population was

The shores of San Francisco were jammed with ships delivering people bound for California's mining camps.

about 100,000. Most people were recent arrivals. Californians asked the U.S. government for statehood. On September 9, 1850, Congress admitted California as the thirty-first state.

The gold rush also sped up the creation and growth of many towns. San Francisco's population was just eight hundred at the start of 1848. After the gold rush began, San Francisco grew quickly. Ships carrying gold

## Women and the Gold Rush

Nearly all of the miners were men, so there was a shortage of women in gold rush days. By 1850, only about one-tenth of California's non-Indian population was female. Many of the women and girls were miners' wives and daughters who had joined them in California.

seekers landed there. The town also became the prospectors' main supply center. By 1850, San Francisco was home to about 40,000 people. Its population had multiplied by fifty in just two years—thanks to gold.

Sacramento traces its roots to 1839, when John Sutter built Sutter's Fort there. It was not actually a town until a decade later, when it became a supply center and stopping-off point for Forty-Niners. By 1850, Sacramento had seven thousand people. Four years later, in 1854, Sacramento became the state **capital**, as it still is today.

Many other California cities and towns began as gold rush communities between 1848 and 1850. They include Auburn, Eureka, Yuba City, Stockton, Nevada City, Placerville (once called Hangtown), Oroville, Sonora, and Benicia.

Jobs in a gold mine included "mucking," or shoveling broken rock (muck) into carts for removal to the surface.

# CHAPTER SIX

# The Gold Rush Ends

In the 1850s gold mining changed in California. The days of the lone miner came to an end. Instead, companies ran big mining operations. Most individual prospectors went to work for these firms. The rest stopped mining for gold completely.

Mining methods also changed. Instead of using pans or cradles, miners dug tunnels and went underground to search for gold. The tunnels were dangerous. Sometimes they collapsed and killed the miners inside.

Mine operators began to do a great deal of **hydraulic gold mining**. Miners aimed high-powered blasts of water at the ground to uncover gold.

## A Deadly Discovery

Centuries ago, about 300,000 Native Americans lived in California. By the mid-1800s, there were only about half that many. The huge population change of the California Gold Rush hurt the American Indians. Thousands died of diseases brought in by the outsiders. Thousands more were killed in fights with white people. Others were pushed out of California. By 1900, only about 16,000 Native Americans remained in the Golden State.

The big problem with hydraulic mining was that it hurt the environment. The powerful equipment washed away entire hillsides and flooded woodlands and farms.

The California Gold Rush ended around 1857. By this time, much of the state's gold was gone. At least $400 million in gold was found in California between 1848 and 1857. That would amount to $10 billion today. Many miners left no record of their discoveries, however. The true amount of gold mined in the California Gold Rush will never be known.

What happened to the hundreds of thousands of miners who went to California during the gold rush? Some returned to their original homes. Others went on to prospect in places like Nevada, where a rich silver deposit was discovered in 1859.

Hydraulic miners in Nevada County using water cannons to blast away rock, 1866

This 1903 photograph shows a steam harvester cutting through a California wheat field.

Many former miners realized that California had other treasures besides gold. It had lovely scenery, from its seashore to its snow-capped mountains. It had warm weather and rich soil. Thousands of ex-miners stayed in California to farm, to ranch, and to pursue other kinds of work. By 1890, California had more than 1.2 million people. The state ranked twenty-second in population among the forty-four states. This was impressive for a state that was only forty years old.

Today, the Golden State's population is more than thirty-six million. No other state has as many people. California is also the leading state for both farming and **manufacturing**. It all began with the gold rush, when a gleaming yellow metal attracted people from around the world to California.

# Glossary

**archaeologist**—A scientist who studies the remains of people and cultures.

**capital**—A place where laws for a nation or state are made.

**cradles**—Devices that separate gold from other materials; also called rockers.

**crucial**—Very important.

**hydraulic gold mining**—The use of high-powered blasts of water to uncover gold.

**manufacturing**—The making of products.

**merchants**—People who buy and sell goods.

**nuggets**—Solid lumps of gold or other materials.

**panned**—Searched for gold by collecting and washing material in a pan.

**placer mining**—The process of searching streambeds for loose gold.

**population**—The number of people in a place.

**profit**—A gain; an amount of money greater than the amount a person has spent on a business venture or project.

**prospectors**—People who search for gold or other valuable materials.

**substance**—A type of material.

**territories**—Areas of land that belong to a country.

# Timeline

**1542**—Juan Rodriguez Cabrillo explores California's coast for Spain

**1769**—Spaniards found San Diego, California's first European settlement

**1776**—Spaniards found San Francisco

**1821**—Mexico frees itself from Spain

**1822**—Mexico takes control of California

**1846**—The United States goes to war with Mexico

**1848—January 24:** James Marshall discovers gold at John Sutter's sawmill; the California Gold Rush begins
**February 2:** By the Treaty of Guadalupe Hidalgo, Mexico gives the United States a huge amount of land, including California

*1542*          *1846*          *1848*

**1849**—About 85,000 Forty-Niners flock to California in search of gold

**1857**—The California Gold Rush is mostly over

**1860**—California's population reaches 380,000

**1850—September 9:** California becomes the thirty-first state in the United States

**1998**—It is the 150th anniversary of Marshall's discovery of gold in California

**1854**—Sacramento becomes California's state capital; the San Francisco Mint opens

**2000**—California celebrates 150 years of statehood

*1849*                    *1857*          *2000*

# Further Information

**B O O K S**

Crewe, Sabrina, and Michael V. Uschan. *The California Gold Rush*. Milwaukee: Gareth Stevens, 2003.

Dolan, Edward F. *The California Gold Rush*. New York: Benchmark Books, 2003.

Isaacs, Sally Senzell. *The Gold Rush*. Chicago: Heinemann Library, 2004.

Thompson, Linda. *The California Gold Rush*. Vero Beach, FL: Rourke, 2005.

## WEB SITES

This site has an excellent description of various aspects of the gold rush:
http://www.kidport.com/REFLIB/UsaHistory/CalGoldRush/CalGoldRush.htm

Look at this site for many interesting facts about the gold rush:
http://www.pbskids.org/wayback/goldrush/features.html

This site provides an excellent biography of James Marshall:
http://www.pbs.org/weta/thewest/people/i_r/marshall.htm

Here you will find an excellent biography of John Sutter:
http://www.pbs.org/weta/thewest/people/s_z/sutter.htm

# Bibliography

Axon, Gordon V. *The California Gold Rush*. New York: Mason/Charter, 1976.

Bernstein, Peter L. *The Power of Gold: The History of an Obsession*. New York: Wiley, 2000.

Brands, H. W. *The Age of Gold: The California Gold Rush and the New American Dream*. New York: Doubleday, 2002.

Holliday, J. S. *Rush for Riches: Gold Fever and the Making of California*. Oakland and Berkeley, CA: Oakland Museum of California and the University of California Press, 1999.

Wells, Evelyn, and Harry C. Peterson. *The '49ers*. Garden City, NY: Doubleday, 1949.

# Index

Page numbers in **boldface** are illustrations.

# About the Author

Dennis Fradin is the author of 150 books, some of them written with his wife, Judith Bloom Fradin. Their book for Clarion, *The Power of One: Daisy Bates and the Little Rock Nine*, was named a Golden Kite Honor Book. Another of Dennis's well-known books is *Let It Begin Here! Lexington & Concord: First Battles of the American Revolution*, published by Walker. Other recent books by the Fradins include *Jane Addams: Champion of Democracy* for Clarion and *5,000 Miles to Freedom: Ellen and William Craft's Flight from Slavery* for National Geographic Children's Books. Their current project for National Geographic is the *Witness to Disaster* series about natural disasters. *Turning Points in U.S. History* is Dennis's first series for Marshall Cavendish Benchmark. The Fradins have three grown children and five grandchildren.